THE TEXAS LINK TO
Sausage Making

LARRY BURRIER

EAKIN PRESS ⭐ Austin, Texas

For CIP
information,
please access:
www.loc.gov

FIRST EDITION
Copyright © 2002
By Larry Burrier
Published in the United States of America
By Eakin Press
A Division of Sunbelt Media, Inc.
P.O. Drawer 90159 ☐ Austin, Texas 78709-0159
email: sales@eakinpress.com
☐ website: www.eakinpress.com ☐
ALL RIGHTS RESERVED.

1   2   3   4   5   6   7   8   9
1-57168-745-9

Contents

*Old World European sausage making the way it was
supposed to be—plain and simple—
from the heart of "The Barbecue Capital of Texas"
in Lockhart, Texas*

These sausage recipes, old and new, come to you through our family of French/German/Irish descendants who settled in Texas in the early 1800s, bringing with them the expert knowledge of Old World sausage making to be handed down through generations and shared with friends and neighbors.

Larry Burrier and the Burrier Family

INTRODUCTION
The History of Sausage

Today's art of sausage making has changed very little from its beginnings some 5,000 years ago, when the Sumarians were said to have invented this ingenious method of preserving meat. The name *sausage* is derived from the Latin word *salsus*, meaning salted or preserved.

But too little homage is paid to the importance of sausage and the role it played in sustaining our ancestors as they struggled to endure the bitter European winters and sweltering summers.

Each region created its own type of sausage, blending herbs and spices native to that country or region. Some ancient sausage recipes have even been found in a cookbook dated 228 A.D.!

While the method of production has altered only slightly, the varieties are nearly unlimited and distinctly unique to each country, with names that you're bound to recognize: bologna from Bologna, Italy; salami from Salamis; Berliner from Germany; and Lyons from Lyons, France. And let's not forget the American Indians, who made sausage patties from buffalo and venison.

Eventually Europeans migrated to America, introducing their sausage recipes. Small butcher shops soon emerged, some of which grew into leading manufacturers of the twenty-first century, and all of whom are indebted to the pioneers of 900 B.C.

And so, from the Burrier family of French, German and Irish heritage, we pass along our own European/American sausage recipes and sausage-making tradition for you to enjoy.

CHAPTER I
Preparation and General Instructions

In addition to having good flavor, homemade beef, pork or venison sausage provides an excellent source of protein, B vitamins, and minerals. It's also very economical, considering most store-bought varieties cost far more than home-produced sausage.

Another advantage to making sausage at home is that you are in control of the entire process. Critical fat-to-lean ratios as well as salt and preservatives can be modified to your personal taste or health requirements. Commercial sausage producers have little choice in these matters, adding such preservatives as monosodium glutamate, potassium sorbate, and silcon dioxide into their sausage-making process to preserve color, retard rancidity, and extend shelf life.

Proper Field Dressing
and Processing of Venison

Most people claim that deer meat has a *"gamey"* or *"wild"* taste. This isn't necessarily true. There is very little, if any, wild or gamey taste if proper care is taken promptly after the deer is downed.

To eliminate any gamey flavor after downing a buck, first cut away the tarsal glands found on the inside hock of the rear legs. Make sure that you clean your knife and hands with a mixture of vinegar-water before proceeding with any further field processing.

Next, remove all internal organs, being careful not to puncture or burst any of these. Flush the internal cavity with clean water, if available.

Once back at deer camp, hang the deer and skin it immediately. Mix one gallon of vinegar with two gallons of water, and with either a rag or nylon hand-brush, scrub the entire outside of the carcass, until all foreign matter is removed. Once again, scrub the inside cavity, removing any remaining blood and filament. When properly cleaned, the inside should be a pale pink color.

If any fat is left on the hindquarters, remove at once, discarding all fatty tissue removed.

Never use venison fat in sausage.

For transporting and to avoid getting any dirt or

insects on the deer carcass, cover it with a game bag, usually made of cotton cheesecloth or other like material.

Should the weather turn warmer and you intend to stay at deer camp, or if you are ready to transport the deer carcass home, cut your deer into quarters and store in an ice-filled cooler. If you choose to store your deer, place it in a cold-storage locker that maintains a temperature of 33–36 degrees Fahrenheit.

Upon returning home, begin cutting, taking extra care to remove all tallow, fat, and gristle from the meat. Anything that isn't rich, lean meat should be discarded.

A lot of people assume sausage is made from inferior meats. Not so! If you use well-cleaned, lean meat, with proper amounts of pork and fat, your attempt at homemade sausage making will be a rewarding experience, resulting in a top-grade product.

Casings

All of the listed casings can be purchased from meat markets, meat market supply stores, or butcher shops.

Natural Hog Casing

Natural casings commonly used for sausage making are hog casings. Although they are sold in various amounts and sizes, hog casings are generally sold in "hanks," one set being 100 yards, which will normally yield 100 pounds of sausage, depending on how you fill or stuff it.

Natural casings come packed in a salt solution. Prior to use, rinse the casings and then place them in a bowl of water for overnight storage in the refrigerator.

Natural Sheep Casing

Sheep casing is also sold in "hanks," just as the hog casing, but because these are smaller in diameter, they will yield about 50-70 pounds of sausage. These casings are also packed in a salt solution and should be rinsed and placed in a bowl of water in the refrigerator overnight before use.

Sheep casings are best used for *Breakfast Links, Wieners, Franks, Brown-and-Serve Breakfast Links,* or *"CopyCat Slim Jims."*

Fibrous Casing

Fibrous casings are a larger, "manufactured" casing, about 2x24 inches. They are used for *Salami, Summer Sausage, or Sausage Rolls.*

The fibrous casing should always be soaked in warm water for about 20 minutes prior to use. This will soften the casing and make it easier to work with.

Curing Salts

Curing salts are used in sausage making to preserve the meat and meat color and to prevent food poisoning.

Commercial Cures
Commercial cure is a mixture of *salt, monosodium glutamate,* and *nitrate.* Regulated by the United States Department of Agriculture, cure manufacturers are responsible for maintaining the appropriate measures set forth by the Federal Food Administrators, insuring no more than 200 parts per million of residual nitrate.

Curing salt contains *dextrose, sodium nitrate,* and *glycerin.*

Cure usage should be at the rate of 4 ounces (20 teaspoons) per 100 pounds of meat, or 1 ounce (5 teaspoons) per 25 pounds of meat, or 1 teaspoon per 5 pounds of meat.

My preference is *Morton's Curing Salt.*

Items Needed for Sausage Making

To make homemade sausage, you'll need clean, tallow-free venison, or lean fat-free beef, as well as pork butt that has a meat-to-fat ratio of about 80% lean meat and 20% fat.

Most food stores and meat markets will sell pork butt, pre-cut at 80/20.

Necessary equipment includes *several sharp knives, cutting board, measuring cups and spoons, mixing tub or bowls*, and a *meat grinder or food processor*. The meat grinder or food processor should be preferably equipped with $\frac{1}{8}$ inch and $\frac{3}{8}$ inch grinding plates and assorted sausage horns ($\frac{1}{2}$ inch and $\frac{3}{4}$ inch) for stuffing sausage into casing.

The best types of casings are natural casings because they are easiest to use, especially for the beginner.

Casings should be thoroughly cleaned by rinsing in cold water and then soaked overnight in a refrigerator, prior to using. Leftover casings can be repacked in a salt solution and frozen until needed.

One set of hog casing will yield approximately 100 pounds of sausage.

Rinse casing in cold water before stuffing. Keep casing in water until needed.

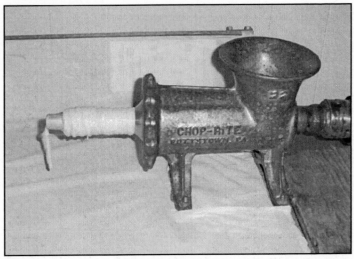

Slide hog casing onto the sausage funnel, leaving approximately 2 inches of casing hanging off the end of the funnel. Tie a knot at the end of the casing.

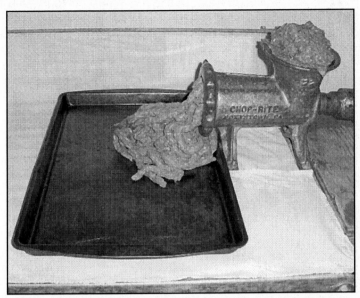

Grind the meat mixture through a ³/₈-inch grinding plate.

Combine dry ingredients and meat mixture. Mix and knead thoroughly.

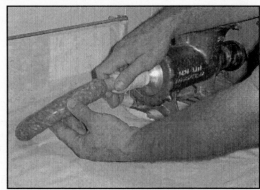

Stuff seasoned mixture into the natural hog casing. Fill the casing snugly, but not so tightly that it will burst the casing.

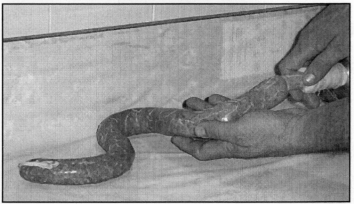

Twist link and tie-off into desired size.

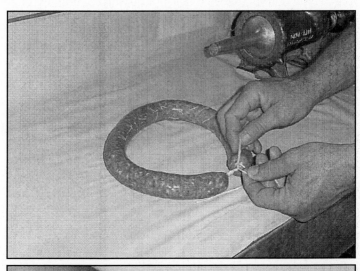

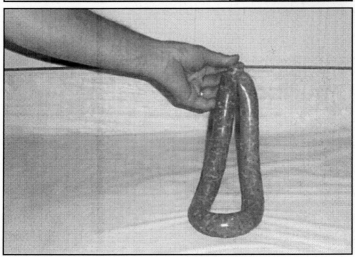

Tie link into horseshoe-shaped links if desired.

Preparing Ingredients for Sausage

Choose one of the following recipes, gather all of the ingredients, and set aside. Weigh out the appropriate amounts of venison or lean beef and pork butt.

Remember to use the best quality beef or pork for a better-finished product. For venison, refer to pages 3-4, on the proper way to prepare for sausage use. Always use clean, fat, and tallow-free venison.

Cut meat into pieces to accommodate your grinder or food processor. Some grinders will handle larger pieces than others will. Through a ³/₈ inch grinding plate, grind all of your meats together, place in a large container, and mix thoroughly.

Each recipe in this book will list a variety of required *dry mixture* ingredients, which should be measured, combined, and mixed thoroughly; add only one-half of this dry mixture to the ground meat, mixing and kneading well. The next step will be to add the remaining dry ingredients to the meat mixture, as well as the appropriate amount of water, which will make the mixing process easier. Continue to mix and knead the mixture until all ingredients are thoroughly blended.

After all of the ingredients have been mixed, place them in the refrigerator to chill for several hours.

Stuffing the Casing

Now let's have some fun! Attach the appropriately sized sausage horn (funnel) onto your grinder or food processor (horns should be slightly smaller than the desired casing). Use the $^3/_4$ inch size horn for hog casing, to prevent the casing from tearing. Have the casing soaking in a bowl of water until you're ready to begin, then remove one section from the water at a time.

Next, fill the grinding stuffer or food processor with some of the seasoned meat and turn the switch on until the meat mixture begins exiting the horn. This allows the meat to push any air out of the horn, preventing air pockets in your casing.

Turn off the grinder and begin sliding a length of casing over the horn, continuing until the end of the casing is at the opening of the horn. Now use a 6-inch-long piece of cotton twine to tie off the casing end. You are now ready to turn on your grinder and begin stuffing the seasoned meat into the casing.

Your objective will be to maintain the diameter of sausage you desire (1 inch to $1^1/_4$ inch) throughout the entire length, without bursting the casing. If you're unsure as to whether or not the casing is filled too tightly, cut off the first three feet of stuffed sausage and attempt to form a horseshoe-shaped link, or cut a 12- to 14-inch link—if the casing easily splits when tied off, the links are too tightly filled. In this case, you'll want to adjust your stuffing technique accordingly by the amount of casing you release while feeding meat through the stuffer. The less casing you release, the tighter the fill; the more casing you release, the less-filled the casing becomes.

Stuff the entire length of casing first, then form and tie off links in desired sizes and shapes. Again, one set of hog casing will yield about 100 pounds of sausage.

Your fresh homemade sausage is now ready for freezing or cooking.

If you choose to smoke your sausage before freezing, refer to pages 21-22, for easy to follow directions on *Smoking and Curing Sausage.*

Cooking Sausage

Outdoor Grilling

If you choose to cook on a barbecue grill, using natural woods such as oak, mesquite or pecan, first burn the wood down to smoldering coals and then place the sausage on the grill. Or you may want to use commercial charcoal from the grocery store.

Either way, place the meat 10-12 inches to the side of the smoldering coals, so that your meat cooks slowly and doesn't burn.

If you are using a propane grill, light only one side of the burner and place the sausage on the unlit side of the grill.

Cook for 15-20 minutes, turning often to brown both sides.

Oven Broiling

Adjust your oven rack 6-10 inches from the broiling element. Set the thermostat to broil and place sausage on a cookie sheet. You may want to brush the meat with your favorite barbecue sauce. Allow sausage to brown on one side before turning, completing the broiling process in approximately 8-10 minutes.

Boiled Sausage

Using an iron skillet, add 2 inches of water, allowing it to come to a boil before adding sausage.

Cook meat for 8-10 minutes on one side, carefully turning on the opposite side without puncturing, to continue cooking until the sausage is thoroughly cooked.

Pan Frying
Slice sausage in half lengthwise. Preheat 3-4 tablespoons of cooking oil in a skillet and add sausage, turning frequently until browned on both sides, approximately 8-10 minutes.

Smoking and Curing Sausage

The best method for smoking and curing meat is *Cold Smoking*. This process lessens the risk of burning the sausage.

First, choose the type of wood you would like to use. My favorite is seasoned *oak*; my second choice is *mesquite* because of its availability in Texas and the flavor it lends; and my third choice is *pecan* wood for a mellow, smoked flavor.

Burn the wood down to smoldering coals. Have wood chips soaking in water to keep moist and add small portions at a time, to keep the burning coals active. **Never allow the coals to flame.** Temperature should be maintained between 90 and 100 degrees Fahrenheit.

Using a metal rod, hang the sausage links one inch apart inside the smoker, never allowing the links to touch, which may cause an uneven smoke distribution.

There are two important chemicals found in wood smoke; one is formaldehyde and the other is acetic acid. Both of these chemicals act as preservatives. The longer the smoke exposure, the more preservatives will be absorbed. However, a minimum or maximum amount of smoke has very little to do with the finished product.

Smoked sausage links that are to be cured for *drying* should be smoked for approximately 5-8 hours. After the smoking process is complete, hang sausage in a cool room that maintains a temperature between 40-55 degrees for a period of 18-21 days, depending on the degree of dryness you desire.

While hanging, if mold forms on links, wipe each link with a vinegar-soaked towel to kill and remove the mold.

Sausage that will be used for cooking should be smoked for 2-3 hours, for a light smoked flavor. Afterward, double-wrap each link in freezer paper and keep frozen until needed.

CHAPTER 2
Sausage Recipes

Specific directions for grinding, measuring/ combining, and cooking/smoking are covered in detail on pages 15-22.

Old-Fashioned German Sausage

(30 pounds)

15 pounds Lean Beef or Venison

15 pounds Pork Butt

15 tablespoons Salt

6 teaspoons Curing Salt

9 tablespoons Coarse Black Pepper

6 tablespoons Paprika

6 tablespoons Garlic Granules

3 tablespoons Crushed Red Chili Pepper

6 tablespoons Ground Yellow Mustard Seed

3 cups Nonfat Dry Milk

3 cups Water

Directions

(1) Grind meat through medium grinding plate ($^3/_8$ inch).

(2) Measure and combine dry ingredients.

(3) Combine ground meat and dry ingredients. Add water and mix thoroughly.

(4) Stuff casing with seasoned mixture.

(5) Cook or smoke sausage.

German Garlic Sausage

(30 pounds)

21 pounds Lean Beef or Venison

9 pounds Pork Butt

10 tablespoons Garlic Granules

12 tablespoons Salt

3 teaspoons Nutmeg

3 teaspoons Cinnamon

6 tablespoons Paprika

3 teaspoons Cloves

6 tablespoons Coarse Black Pepper

3 cups Water

3 cups Nonfat Dry Milk

Directions

(1) Grind meat through a ³/₈ inch grinding plate.

(2) Measure and combine all dry ingredients.

(3) Combine ground meat and dry ingredients. Add water and mix thoroughly.

(4) Stuff casing with seasoned mixture.

(5) Fry, broil, bake or grill, the same as any link sausage.

German Potato Sausage

(10 pounds)

5$\frac{1}{2}$ pounds Lean Beef or Venison

2$\frac{1}{2}$ pounds Pork Butt

4$\frac{1}{2}$ tablespoons Salt

$\frac{3}{4}$ teaspoon Nutmeg

$\frac{3}{4}$ tablespoon White Pepper

1 tablespoon Black Pepper

$\frac{3}{4}$ teaspoon Allspice

$\frac{3}{4}$ teaspoon Ginger

2 cups Green Onions—chopped

2 pounds Potatoes—lightly boiled and chopped

2 cups Nonfat Dry Milk

1 cup Water

Directions

(1) Grind meat and potatoes through $\frac{3}{8}$ inch grinding plate.
(2) Measure and combine dry ingredients.
(3) Combine ground meat and dry ingredients. Add water and mix thoroughly.
(4) Stuff casing with seasoned mixture.
(5) Fry, broil, bake or grill, the same as any link sausage.

German Apple Sausage

(9 pounds)

3³/₄ pounds Lean Beef or Venison

3³/₄ pounds Pork Butt (80/20)

1¹/₂ pounds Tart Green Apples—peeled

2 tablespoons Salt

2 tablespoons Coriander

3 tablespoons Garlic Granules

3 tablespoons Paprika

2¹/₂ tablespoons Coarse Black Pepper

4 tablespoons Parsley Flakes

1¹/₂ tablespoons Cinnamon

³/₄ cup Water

1¹/₂ cups Nonfat Dry Milk

Directions

(1) Grind meats and apples through a ³/₈ inch grinding plate.

(2) Measure and combine all dry ingredients.

(3) Combine ground meat and apple mixture with dry ingredients. Add water and mix thoroughly.

(4) Stuff casing with seasoned mixture.

(5) Fry, broil, bake or grill, the same as any link sausage.

German Beerwurst Sausage

(15 pounds)

9 pounds Lean Beef or Venison

6 pounds Pork Butt

3 teaspoons Curing Salt

8 tablespoons Salt

4$\frac{1}{2}$ tablespoons Whole Fennel Seed

4$\frac{1}{2}$ tablespoons Crushed Red Chili Pepper

4$\frac{1}{2}$ tablespoons Dried Bell Pepper Flakes

1$\frac{1}{2}$ tablespoons Chili Powder

1$\frac{1}{2}$ tablespoons Ground Coriander Seed

4$\frac{1}{2}$ tablespoons Cayenne Pepper

1$\frac{1}{2}$ cups Nonfat Dry Milk

1$\frac{1}{2}$ cups Water

Directions

(1) Grind meat through a $\frac{3}{8}$ grinding plate.

(2) Measure and combine dry ingredients.

(3) Combine ground meat and dry ingredients. Add water and mix thoroughly.

(4) Stuff casing with seasoned mixture.

(5) Cook or smoke sausage.

German Liverwurst Sausage

(10 pounds)

4 pounds Beef or Venison Hearts

4 pounds Beef or Venison Liver

3 pounds Pork Butt

5 tablespoons Salt

2 teaspoons Curing Salt

2 teaspoons Marjoram

2 teaspoons Ginger

2 teaspoons Nutmeg

2 tablespoons Onion Powder

6 teaspoons White Pepper

1 cup Water

2 cups Nonfat Dry Milk

Directions

(1) Combine venison or beef hearts and liver in a large boiling pot. Slow-boil for about $2^{1}/_{2}$ hours. Drain and let cool.

(2) Grind the cooked hearts and liver with pork butt, using a fine ($^{1}/_{8}$ inch) grinding plate.

(3) Measure and combine all dry ingredients in a large mixing bowl. Add water to the meat mixture, mixing and kneading thoroughly.

(4) Grind mixture a second time, using a medium ($^{3}/_{8}$ inch) grinding plate.

(5) Stuff seasoned meat mixture into hog casings, tie off in horseshoe-shaped links.

(6) Let cure overnight in refrigerator.

(7) Place sausage into a preheated pot of water with a water temperature of 170 degrees. Simmer (***do not boil***) until internal temperature reaches 155 degrees.

(8) Remove sausage from hot water and shower with cold water until cool to the touch.

(9) Lay sausage on a towel until dry. Once dry, it is ready to eat.

German Bratwurst

(15 pounds)

10$\frac{1}{2}$ pounds Lean Beef

4$\frac{1}{2}$ pounds Pork Butt

6 tablespoons Salt

3 Whole Eggs

4$\frac{1}{2}$ tablespoons Sugar

2 teaspoons Black Pepper

2 teaspoons White Pepper

1$\frac{1}{2}$ teaspoons Nutmeg

6 tablespoons Parsley Flakes

1$\frac{1}{2}$ teaspoons Mace

1$\frac{1}{2}$ teaspoons Ginger

3 cups Nonfat Dry Milk

1$\frac{1}{2}$ cups Water

Directions

(1) Grind meat and pork together through a small ($\frac{1}{8}$ inch) grinding plate.

(2) Measure and combine dry ingredients.

(3) Combine ground meat and dry ingredients. Add water and mix thoroughly.

(4) Stuff seasoned mixture into hog casing and tie-off into 6- to 8-inch links. Refrigerate.

(5) Fry, bake, broil or grill, the same as any link sausage.

German Bockwurst

(15 pounds)

7¹/₂ pounds Lean Beef

7¹/₂ pounds Pork Butt

3 teaspoons Mace

3 teaspoons Allspice

6 teaspoons Celery Seed

1¹/₂ teaspoons Ground Coriander

1¹/₂ teaspoons Ginger

7¹/₂ tablespoons White Pepper

6 Whole Eggs

7¹/₂ tablespoons Salt

12 Green Onions—diced

12 Minced Garlic Cloves

1¹/₂ cups Water

6 cups Nonfat Dry Milk

Directions

(I) Grind meat and pork together through a small (¹/₈ inch) grinding plate.

(2) Measure and combine dry ingredients.

(3) Combine ground meat and dry ingredients. Add water and mix thoroughly.

(4) Stuff seasoned mixture into hog casings and tie-off into 6- to 8-inch links. Refrigerate.

(5) Fry, bake, broil or grill, the same as any link sausage.

Polish Link Sausage

(20 pounds)

14 pounds Lean Beef or Venison

6 pounds Pork Butt

3 tablespoons Garlic Powder

2 tablespoons Onion Powder

3 tablespoons Coarse Black Pepper

8 tablespoons Salt

5 tablespoons Sugar

4 tablespoons Whole Mustard Seed

3 teaspoons Marjoram

2 tablespoons Crushed Red Chili Pepper

2 cups Nonfat Dry Milk

2 cups Water

Directions

(1) Grind meat through a medium ($^3/_8$ inch) grinding plate.

(2) Measure and combine dry ingredients.

(3) Combine ground meat and dry ingredients. Add water and mix thoroughly.

(4) Stuff casing with seasoned mixture.

(5) Fry, broil, bake or grill, the same as any link sausage.

Kielbasa Link Sausage

(20 pounds)

12 pounds Lean Beef or Venison

8 pounds Pork Butt

10 tablespoons Salt

5 tablespoons Garlic Granules

4 teaspoons Curing Salt

2 tablespoons White Pepper

2 teaspoons Nutmeg

2 teaspoons Cardamon

4 tablespoons Ground Yellow Mustard Seed

2 cups Nonfat Dry Milk

2 cups Water

Directions

(1) Grind meat through a medium ($3/8$ inch) grinding plate.

(2) Measure and combine dry ingredients.

(3) Combine ground meat and dry ingredients. Add water and mix thoroughly.

(4) Stuff casing with seasoned mixture.

(5) Cook or smoke sausage.

Texas-Style Jalapeño Sausage

(20 pounds)

12 pounds Lean Beef or Venison

8 pounds Pork Butt

10 tablespoons Salt

4 teaspoons Curing Salt

6 tablespoons Jalapeño Powder

8 tablespoons Jalapeño Peppers—diced

10 tablespoons Dried Bell Pepper Flakes

2 tablespoons Nutmeg

4 tablespoons Paprika

2 tablespoons Mace

2 cups Nonfat Dry Milk

2 cups Water

Directions

(1) Grind meat through a medium ($^3/_8$ inch) grinding plate.

(2) Measure and combine dry ingredients.

(3) Combine ground meat and dry ingredients. Add water and mix thoroughly.

(4) Stuff casing with seasoned mixture.

(5) Cook or smoke sausage.

Texas-Style Garlic Sausage

(20 pounds)

14 pounds Lean Beef or Venison

6 pounds Pork Butt

6 tablespoons Garlic Granules

4 tablespoons Paprika

8 tablespoons Salt

5 tablespoons Coarse Black Pepper

4 tablespoons Brown Sugar

2 teaspoons Cloves

2 teaspoons Cinnamon

2 teaspoons Nutmeg

2 cups Nonfat Dry Milk

2 cups Water

Directions

(1) Grind meat through a medium (³/₈ inch) grinding plate.

(2) Measure and combine dry ingredients.

(3) Combine ground meat and dry ingredients. Add water and mix thoroughly.

(4) Stuff casing with seasoned mixture.

(5) Fry, broil, bake or grill, the same as any link sausage.

Texas-Style Venison and Bacon Sausage

(10 pounds)

6 pounds Venison

4 pounds Bacon—cooked and crumbled

2 pounds Pork Butt

2 tablespoons Sage

2 tablespoons Black Pepper

2 tablespoons Salt

2 teaspoons Coriander

2 teaspoons Ground Yellow Mustard Seed

3 tablespoons Garlic Granules

2 teaspoons Marjoram

1 cup Nonfat Dry Milk

1 cup Water

Directions

(1) Grind meat through a medium ($^3/_8$ inch) grinding plate.

(2) Measure and combine dry ingredients.

(3) Combine ground meat and dry ingredients. Add water and mix thoroughly.

(4) Stuff casing with seasoned mixture.

(5) Fry, broil, bake or grill, the same as any link sausage.

Texas-Style Black Pepper and Onion Sausage

(20 pounds)

14 pounds Lean Beef or Venison

6 pounds Pork Butt

8 tablespoons Parsley Flakes

8 tablespoons Salt

2 tablespoons Onion Flakes

7 tablespoons Coarse Black Pepper

3 tablespoons Garlic Granules

2 tablespoons Marjoram

6 cups Green Onion—chopped

2 cups Nonfat Dry Milk

2 cups Water

Directions

(1) Grind meat through a medium ($^3/_8$ inch) grinding plate.

(2) Measure and combine dry ingredients.

(3) Combine ground meat and dry ingredients. Add water and mix thoroughly.

(4) Stuff casing with seasoned mixture.

(5) Fry, broil, bake or grill, the same as any link sausage.

Texas-Style Chorizo Sausage

(5 pounds)

$3^{1}/_{2}$ pounds Lean Beef or Venison

$^{3}/_{4}$ pound Pork Butt

$^{3}/_{4}$ pound Pork Fat

1 tablespoon Paprika

$1^{1}/_{2}$ tablespoons Cayenne Pepper

2 tablespoons Salt

2 tablespoons Garlic Granules

1 tablespoon Black Pepper

$^{1}/_{2}$ tablespoon Oregano

$^{1}/_{4}$ cup Vinegar

$^{1}/_{2}$ cup Water

$^{1}/_{4}$ cup Nonfat Dry Milk

Directions

(1) Grind meat through a medium ($^{3}/_{8}$ inch) grinding plate.

(2) Measure and combine dry ingredients.

(3) Combine ground meat and dry ingredients. Add water and mix thoroughly.

(4) Stuff meat mixture into casing and tie-off into 6- to 8-inch links.

(5) Slow-fry sausage, along with scrambled eggs. Serve on Tortillas with your favorite Texas Hot Sauce.

Burrier Family Breakfast Sausage

(5 pounds)

3$\frac{1}{2}$ pounds Lean Beef or Venison

$\frac{3}{4}$ pound Pork Butt

$\frac{3}{4}$ pound Pork Fat

1$\frac{1}{2}$ teaspoons Allspice

1 tablespoon Coarse Ground Black Pepper

I tablespoon Garlic Granules

2$\frac{1}{2}$ tablespoons Salt

1 tablespoon Thyme

1$\frac{1}{2}$ tablespoons Crushed Red Chili Pepper

1 tablespoon Yellow Mustard Seed—ground

1 tablespoon Sage

$\frac{1}{2}$ cup Nonfat Dry Milk

$\frac{1}{2}$ cup Water

Directions

(1) Grind meat through a medium ($\frac{3}{8}$ inch) grinding plate.

(2) Measure and combine dry ingredients.

(3) Combine ground meat and dry ingredients. Add water and mix thoroughly.

(4) Shape sausage into 4-inch-diameter patties. Refrigerate or freeze.

(5) Fry, broil or bake, as you would any breakfast sausage.

Country Breakfast Pan Sausage

(5 pounds)

3¹/₂ pounds Lean Beef or Venison

³/₄ pound Pork Butt

³/₄ pound Pork Fat

1¹/₂ tablespoons Sugar

1 tablespoon Bell Pepper—dried

¹/₂ tablespoon Red Pepper—crushed

2 tablespoons Salt

¹/₂ teaspoon Ginger

¹/₂ teaspoon Cayenne Pepper

³/₄ tablespoon Thyme

¹/₂ teaspoon Nutmeg

1 tablespoon Sage

¹/₃ cup Nonfat Dry Milk

¹/₂ cup Water

Directions

(1) Grind meat through a medium ($^3/_8$ inch) grinding plate.
(2) Measure and combine dry ingredients.
(3) Combine ground meat and dry ingredients. Add water and mix thoroughly.
(4) Shape sausage into 4–inch–diameter patties. Refrigerate or freeze.
(5) Fry, broil or bake, as you would any breakfast sausage.

Farmer's Pan Sausage

(5 pounds)

2$\frac{1}{2}$ pounds Venison

1$\frac{1}{2}$ pounds Bacon—uncooked

1 pound Port Butt

$\frac{3}{4}$ tablespoon Salt

$\frac{3}{4}$ teaspoon Rosemary

$\frac{3}{4}$ teaspoon Thyme

1$\frac{3}{4}$ tablespoons Garlic Granules

2 teaspoons Coarse Black Pepper

1$\frac{3}{4}$ teaspoons Marjoram

4 Eggs—beaten

1$\frac{3}{4}$ cups Bread Crumbs—toasted

$\frac{3}{4}$ cup Beef Broth

$\frac{1}{4}$ cup Water

$\frac{1}{2}$ cup Nonfat Dry Milk

Directions

(1) Grind meat through a medium ($\frac{3}{8}$ inch) grinding plate.

(2) Measure and combine dry ingredients.

(3) Combine ground meat and dry ingredients. Add water and mix thoroughly.

(4) Shape sausage into 4-inch-diameter patties. Refrigerate or freeze.

(5) Fry, broil or bake, as you would any breakfast sausage.

Old-Fashioned Sage Breakfast Sausage

(5 pounds)

3 pounds Lean Beef or Venison

1¹/₂ pounds Pork Butt

¹/₂ pound Pork Fat

2 tablespoons Salt

1 tablespoon Coarse Black Pepper

2 tablespoons Garlic Granules

2 tablespoons Red Chili Pepper—crushed

3 tablespoons Sage

1 tablespoon Ground Yellow Mustard Seed

¹/₂ cup Nonfat Dry Milk

¹/₂ cup Water

Directions

(1) Grind meat through a medium (³/₈ inch) grinding plate.

(2) Measure and combine dry ingredients.

(3) Combine ground meat and dry ingredients. Add water and mix thoroughly.

(4) Shape sausage into 4–inch–diameter patties. Refrigerate or freeze.

(5) Fry, broil or bake, as you would any breakfast sausage.

Texas Cheese Smoky-Links

(5 pounds)

3 pounds Lean Beef or Venison

1 pound Pork Butt

1 pound Pork Fat

1 pound Cheddar Cheese

1$\frac{1}{4}$ tablespoons White Pepper

1$\frac{1}{2}$ tablespoons Black Pepper

1 teaspoon Curing Salt

3 tablespoons Salt

2 tablespoons Garlic Granules

1$\frac{1}{4}$ tablespoons Yellow Mustard Seed—ground

$\frac{1}{2}$ cup Nonfat Dry Milk

$\frac{1}{2}$ cup Water

Directions

(1) Dice cheese and freeze the day before preparing ingredients.

(2) Use sheep casing, which is better-suited for the smaller smoky links.

(3) Grind meat mixture and cheese through a $\frac{3}{8}$ inch grinding plate two separate times.

(4) Measure and combine dry ingredients and add half to the meat mixture, mixing well. Add water and the remaining dry ingredients and mix thoroughly.

(5) Stuff seasoned mixture into sheep casing; twist and tie-off into 3- to 5-inch links.

(6) Fry, bake or broil, as you would any breakfast links.

Ginger Smoky-Links

(5 pounds)

3½ pounds Lean Beef or Venison

1½ pounds Pork Butt

1½ teaspoons White Pepper

1½ teaspoons Black Pepper

4 teaspoons Salt

2 teaspoons Ginger

¼ teaspoon Yellow Mustard Seed—ground

¼ cup Sugar

¼ teaspoon Cinnamon

½ cup Nonfat Dry Milk

½ cup Water

Directions

(1) Use sheep casing since they are better-suited for the smaller smoky links.

(2) Grind meat mixture through a ⅜ inch grinding plate two separate times.

(3) Measure and combine dry ingredients and add half to the meat mixture, mixing well. Add water and the remaining dry ingredients and mix thoroughly.

(4) Stuff seasoned mixture into sheep casing; twist and tie-off into 3- to 5-inch links.

(5) Fry, bake or broil, as you would any breakfast links.

Breakfast Brown-and-Serve Links

(5 pounds)

3 pounds Lean Beef or Venison

1 pound Pork Butt

1 pound Pork Fat

2$\frac{1}{2}$ tablespoons Salt

1 teaspoon Curing Salt

1 teaspoon Ginger

1 tablespoon Sage

1 tablespoon Thyme

1 tablespoon Nutmeg

1 tablespoon Red Chili Peppers—crushed

1 teaspoon White Pepper

$\frac{1}{2}$ cup Nonfat Dry Milk

$\frac{1}{2}$ cup Water

Directions

(1) Use sheep casing since they are better suited for the smaller smoky links.

(2) Grind meat mixture through a $\frac{3}{8}$ inch grinding plate two separate times.

(3) Measure and combine dry ingredients and add half to the meat mixture, mixing well. Add water and the remaining dry ingredients and mix thoroughly.

(4) Stuff seasoned mixture into sheep casing; twist and tie-of into 3- to 5-inch links.

(5) Fry, broil or bake, as you would any breakfast links.

Cajun Boudin Sausage

(10 pounds)

4 pounds Long Grain Rice—cooked

2 pounds Lean Beef or Venison

1 pound Pork Butt

1 pound Pork Liver

5 tablespoons Salt

2 tablespoons Paprika

2 teaspoons Cumin

1 teaspoon Chili Powder

3 teaspoons Cayenne Pepper

$^{1}/_{2}$ teaspoon Red Chili Pepper—crushed

2 bunches Parsley—fresh, chopped

2 bunches Green Onions—chopped

2 cups Nonfat Dry Milk

2 cups Water

Directions

(1) In a large pot, bring meat, pork butt, and pork liver to a quick-boil. Reduce heat and simmer until tender. Remove from heat and drain off water.

(2) Grind cooked meat mixture, using a $^{3}/_{8}$ inch grinding plate. Place ground meat mixture in a large container. Pour in cooked rice along with water and all dry ingredients. Mix and knead thoroughly.

(3) Stuff the seasoned mixture into hog casings and tie-off into 8-10 inch links.

(4) Place links in large boiling pot; cover with water and simmer 20 minutes.

(5) Fry, bake or broil, as you would any sausage.

Cajun Crawfish Boudin Sausage

(10 pounds)

1 pound Lean Beef or Venison
1 pound Pork Butt
2 pounds Crawfish—shelled and cooked
4 pounds Long Grain Rice—cooked
5 tablespoons Salt
2 tablespoons Paprika
2 teaspoons Cumin
1 teaspoon Chili Powder
3 teaspoons Cayenne Pepper
$^1/_2$ teaspoon Red Chili Pepper—crushed
2 bunches Parsley—fresh, chopped
2 bunches Green Onion—chopped
2 cups Nonfat Dry Milk
2 cups Water

Directions

(1) In a large pot, bring meat and pork butt to a quick-boil. Reduce heat and simmer until tender. Remove from heat and drain off water.

(2) Grind cooked meat/crawfish mixture, using a $^3/_8$ inch grinding plate. Place ground meat mixture in a large container. Pour in cooked rice along with water and all dry ingredients. Mix and knead thoroughly.

(3) Stuff the seasoned mixture into hog casings and tie-off into 8- to 10-inch links.

(4) Place links in large boiling pot; cover with water and simmer 20 minutes.

(5) Fry, bake or broil, as you would any sausage.

Cajun Catfish Sausage

(5 pounds)

4 pounds Catfish—uncooked, diced

¼ cup Parsley—fresh, chopped

½ cup Green Onion—chopped

1 teaspoon Dill Weed—dried, whole

2 tablespoons Salt

1 teaspoon Coarse Black Pepper

2 teaspoons Cayenne Pepper

1 tablespoon Garlic Granules

1 16-ounce package Stuffing Mix—plain

1½ cups Milk

3 Eggs

1 cup Nonfat Dry Milk

¼ cup Water

Directions

(1) Combine and mix all dry ingredients.

(2) Combine stuffing mix and milk together in mixing bowl. Let soak for 3 minutes.

(3) Add diced fish and dry ingredients to stuffing mix. Blend thoroughly.

(4) Grind the fish mixture using a ⅜ inch grinding plate.

(5) Stuff seasoned fish mixture into hog casing and tie-off in 8- to 10-inch links.

(6) Place links in a large boiling pot; cover with water and simmer 20 minutes.

(7) Fry, bake or broil, as you would any sausage.

Cajun Creole Sausage

(5 pounds)

3¹/₂ pounds Lean Beef or Venison
1¹/₂ pounds Pork Butt
2 tablespoons Salt
1 tablespoon Paprika
1 tablespoon Coarse Black Pepper
1 tablespoon Red Chili Pepper—crushed
¹/₂ teaspoon Cayenne Pepper
¹/₄ teaspoon Allspice
¹/₄ teaspoon Thyme
¹/₄ teaspoon Sage
3 Onions—medium sized, chopped
4 tablespoons Parsley Flakes
¹/₄ cup Nonfat Dry Milk
¹/₂ cup Water

Directions

(1) Grind meat through a medium (³/₈ inch) grinding plate.
(2) Measure and combine dry ingredients.
(3) Combine ground meat and dry ingredients.
(4) Stuff casing with seasoned mixture.
(5) Fry, broil, bake or grill, the same as any link sausage.

Old-Fashioned Italian Sausage

(5 pounds)

3$\frac{1}{2}$ pounds Lean Beef or Venison
1 pound Pork Butt
$\frac{1}{2}$ pound Pork Fat
1 tablespoon Paprika
2 tablespoons Salt
$\frac{1}{2}$ tablespoon Ground Coriander
1 tablespoon Garlic Granules
1 tablespoon Crushed Red Chili Pepper
2 tablespoons Whole Fennel Seed
1 pound Crushed Tomatoes
1 tablespoon Lemon Juice
6 tablespoons Parmesan Cheese—grated
6 tablespoons Mozzarella Cheese—grated
$\frac{3}{4}$ cup Nonfat Dry Milk
$\frac{1}{4}$ cup Water

Directions

(1) Grind meat and pork, using a $\frac{3}{8}$ inch grinding plate.
(2) Measure and combine dry ingredients.
(3) Combine ground meat, tomatoes, cheese, and dry mix, blending thoroughly.
(4) Stuff casing with seasoned mixture and tie-off into 8- to 10-inch links.
(5) Fry, bake or broil, as you would any sausage.

Italian Bell Pepper Sausage

(5 pounds)

3$\frac{1}{2}$ pounds Lean Beef or Venison

1$\frac{1}{2}$ pounds Pork Butt

2 tablespoons Salt

1 tablespoon Garlic Granules

$\frac{1}{2}$ tablespoon Onion Granules

1$\frac{1}{2}$ tablespoons Fennel Seed—whole

2 tablespoons Paprika

1$\frac{1}{2}$ tablespoons Coarse Black Pepper

1$\frac{1}{2}$ tablespoons Red Chili Pepper—crushed

$\frac{1}{4}$ teaspoon Coriander

$\frac{1}{4}$ teaspoon Thyme

2 tablespoons Bell Pepper—dried flakes

$\frac{1}{2}$ cup Nonfat Dry Milk

$\frac{1}{2}$ cup Water

Directions

(1) Grind meat and pork, using $\frac{3}{8}$ inch grinding plate.

(2) Measure and combine dry ingredients.

(3) Combine ground meat and dry ingredients, mixing thoroughly.

(4) Stuff casing with seasoned mixture and tie-off into 8- to 10-inch links.

(5) Fry, bake or broil, as you would any sausage.

Italian Linquisa Sausage

(5 pounds)

3$\frac{1}{2}$ pounds Lean Beef or Venison

1$\frac{1}{2}$ pounds Pork Butt

2 tablespoons Salt

1 tablespoon Garlic Granules

1 tablespoon Paprika

1$\frac{1}{2}$ tablespoons Sugar

$\frac{1}{2}$ tablespoon Cardamon Seed—ground

2 tablespoons Cider Vinegar

$\frac{1}{2}$ tablespoon Black Pepper

1 teaspoon Red Chili Pepper—crushed

$\frac{1}{4}$ cup Nonfat Dry Milk

$\frac{1}{4}$ cup Water

Directions

(1) Grind meat and pork, using $\frac{3}{8}$ inch grinding plate.

(2) Measure and combine dry ingredients.

(3) Combine ground meat and dry ingredients, mixing thoroughly.

(4) Stuff casing with seasoned mixture and tie-off into 8- to 10-inch links.

(5) Fry, bake or broil, as you would any sausage.

Swedish-Style Sausage

(5 pounds)

2 pounds Lean Beef or Venison

1$\frac{1}{2}$ pounds Pork Butt

1$\frac{1}{2}$ pounds Potatoes—lightly boiled

1$\frac{1}{2}$ cups White Onions—chopped

$\frac{1}{2}$ tablespoon Salt

$\frac{1}{2}$ tablespoon White Pepper

$\frac{1}{2}$ tablespoon Onion Powder

1 teaspoon Allspice

$\frac{1}{2}$ teaspoon Marjoram

$\frac{1}{2}$ tablespoon Coarse Black Pepper

1 cup Nonfat Dry Milk

$\frac{1}{2}$ cup Water

Directions

(1) Grind meat and pork, using $\frac{3}{8}$ inch grinding plate.

(2) Measure and combine dry ingredients.

(3) Combine ground meat and dry ingredients, mixing thoroughly.

(4) Stuff casing with seasoned mixture and tie-off into 8- to 10-inch links.

(5) Fry, bake or broil, as you would any sausage.

Swiss-Style Bratwurst

(5 pounds)

3 pounds Lean Beef or Venison

2 pounds Pork Butt

2 tablespoons Parsley Flakes

1 tablespoon White Pepper

1½ tablespoons Salt

1 tablespoon Onion Flakes

1 teaspoon Ginger

2 teaspoons Mace

2 teaspoons Nutmeg

2 cups Croutons—plain, crumbled

2 cups Nonfat Dry Milk

1 cup Water

Directions

(1) Grind meat and pork, using ⅜ inch grinding plate.

(2) Measure and combine dry ingredients.

(3) Combine ground meat and dry ingredients, mixing thoroughly.

(4) Stuff casing with seasoned mixture and tie-off into 8- to 10-inch links.

(5) Fry, bake or broil, as you would any sausage.

Bavarian-Style Sausage

(5 pounds)

3¹/₂ pounds Lean Beef or Venison

1 pound Pork Butt

¹/₂ pound Pork Fat

2¹/₂ tablespoons Salt

¹/₂ teaspoon Mace

¹/₂ teaspoon Nutmeg

¹/₂ cup Parsley Flakes

1 tablespoon White Pepper

¹/₂ teaspoon Black Pepper

¹/₂ teaspoon Garlic Powder

¹/₂ cup White Onion—chopped

¹/₂ cup Red Onion—chopped

¹/₂ cup Chives—chopped

2 cups Nonfat Dry Milk

¹/₂ cup Water

Directions

(1) Grind meat and pork, using ³/₈ inch grinding plates.

(2) Measure and combine dry ingredients.

(3) Combine ground meat and dry ingredients, mixing thoroughly.

(4) Stuff casing with seasoned mixture and tie-of into 8- to 10-inch links.

(5) Fry, bake or broil, as you would any sausage.

Greek-Style Sausage

(5 pounds)

3$\frac{1}{2}$ pounds Lean Beef or Venison

1$\frac{1}{2}$ pounds Pork Butt

1 tablespoon Coarse Black Pepper

2 tablespoons Salt

3 teaspoons Garlic Granules

1$\frac{1}{2}$ tablespoons Marjoram

1 teaspoon Allspice

1 teaspoon Oregano

$\frac{1}{2}$ cup Parsley Flakes

1 cup Onions—chopped

1 tablespoon Thyme

$\frac{1}{4}$ cup Nonfat Dry Milk

$\frac{1}{2}$ cup Water

Directions

(1) Grind meat and pork, using $\frac{3}{8}$ inch grinding plate.

(2) Measure and combine dry ingredients.

(3) Combine ground meat and dry ingredients, mixing thoroughly.

(4) Stuff casing with seasoned mixture and tie-off into 8- to 10-inch links.

(5) Fry, bake or broil, as you would any sausage.

CHAPTER 3
Homemade Cold Cuts and Lunch Meats

Homemade cold cuts or lunch meats seem to be a thing of the past. Unlike sausage, cold cuts are very seldom made at home, and yet with a little work and the same basic equipment used for sausage making, you'll be delighted in producing your own cold cuts!

Unlike sausage, lunch meats or cold cuts use a *fibrous casing* and must be cooked before storing.

The fibrous casing can usually be found at butcher shops, meat markets, or meat market suppliers. They come in 24-inch lengths and are 2-3 inches in diameter.

Before using, the casing should be soaked in warm water for about 20 minutes; this will soften the casing and make it easier to work with.

The technique for stuffing a fibrous casing is the same as used with natural casings (listed on pages 17-18).

Soak fibrous casing for 20 minutes prior to using; this will make the casing easier to work with.

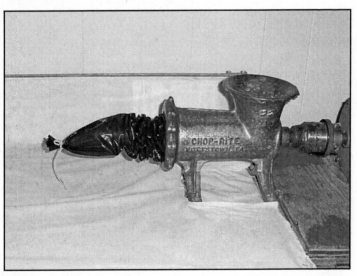

Slide the fibrous casing over the sausage funnel. Squeeze the casing firmly against the funnel with your hand.

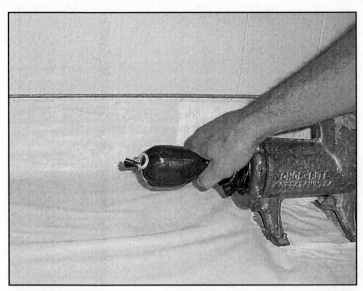

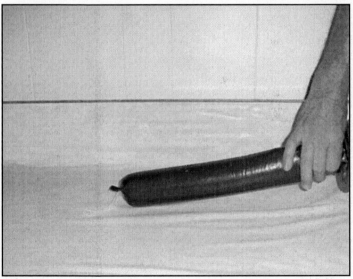

While continuing to squeeze the casing against the funnel, begin to fill the casing. Continue filling until about 1 inch of the casing remains unfilled.

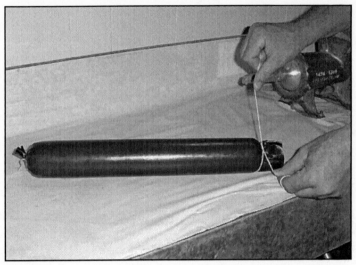

Hold the end of the casing and place an 8-inch piece of twine around the end and tie-off.

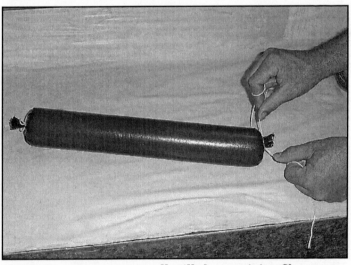

Finished summer sausage roll. Fill the remaining fibrous casings with meat mixture. Once filled, they are ready to cook. Sausage is fully cooked when the internal temperature reaches 150–155 degrees.

How to Cook Cold Cuts

Preheat the oven at its lowest setting, with the door slightly opened. Place the oven rack to the farthest point *away from the heating element*.

Place your product on the oven rack to begin the drying process. When the product is dry to the touch, about 1 hour, reset your oven temperature to 155 degrees. Use an oven thermometer to check the temperature, and if needed, slightly open the oven door to maintain the heat setting. Leave the temperature at 155 degrees for 1 hour, then readjust the oven temperature to 170 degrees.

The sausage product will eventually begin to turn a reddish brown color.

Using a meat thermometer, insert it into the end of the sausage roll. When the internal temperature reaches 150-155 degrees, remove the meat from the oven. If you have several meat rolls in the oven, remove them all.

Submerge the meat products into a hot water bath of 170 degrees for approximately 20 minutes, then place in a cold water bath for 5-6 minutes, or until cool to the touch. This keeps the product from shriveling.

Set a dry towel on the counter and place the meat on the towel, allowing to dry at room temperature and turning occasionally. Once the meat has cooled, it will take on a richer, darker color. It is now ready to eat!

Unused meat products should be double-wrapped and stored in the freezer until needed.

Texas-Style Summer Sausage

(20 pounds)

16 pounds Lean Beef or Venison

4 pounds Pork Butt

2 tablespoons White Pepper

4 tablespoons Yellow Mustard Seed—ground

3 tablespoons Coarse Black Pepper

2 teaspoons Coriander Seed—ground

3 teaspoons Garlic Granules

10 tablespoons Salt

4 teaspoons Curing Salt

6 tablespoons Sugar

4 cups Nonfat Dry Milk

2 cups Water

Directions

(1) Grind meat through a ³/₈ inch grinding plate.

(2) Measure and combine dry ingredients.

(3) Combine meat mixture and dry ingredients in large container and mix well. Next, add water, again mixing and kneading thoroughly.

(4) Re-grind mixture through a ³/₈ inch grinding plate.

(5) Stuff seasoned mixture into 2x24-inch *fibrous casings, previously soaked for 20 minutes.*

(6) Cook sausage according to instructions on *pages 65-66.* Sausage is fully cooked when internal temperature reaches 150–155 degrees.

Texas Style Jalapeño and Cheese Summer Sausage

(20 pounds)

14 pounds Lean Beef or Venison

4 pounds Pork Butt

2 pounds Cheddar Cheese

5 tablespoons Jalapeño Flakes

4 tablespoons Red Chili Pepper—crushed

1 cup Fresh Jalapeño Pepper—remove seeds and dice

10 tablespoons Salt

4 teaspoons Curing Salt

4 tablespoons Mustard Seed—ground

3 teaspoons Garlic Granules

2 teaspoons Coriander Seed—ground

2 tablespoons Coarse Ground Black Pepper

2 tablespoons White Pepper

2 cups Nonfat Dry Milk

2 cups Water

Directions

The day before making sausage, dice and freeze cheddar cheese.

(1) Grind meats through a ³/₈ inch grinding plate.

(2) Measure and combine dry ingredients.

(3) Combine meat mixture, dry ingredients and cheese in large container and mix well. Next, add water and again mix and knead thoroughly.

(4) Re-grind mixture through a ³/₈ inch grinding plate.

(5) Stuff seasoned mixture into 2x24-inch *fibrous casings, previously soaked for 20 minutes.*

(6) Cook sausage according to instructions on *pages 65-66.* Sausage is fully cooked when internal temperature reaches 150-155 degrees.

Texas-Style Salami

(20 pounds)

16 pounds Lean Beef or Venison

4 pounds Pork Butt

4 tablespoons White Pepper

7 tablespoons Pepper Corn—whole

4 tablespoons Anise Seed—whole

4 tablespoons Garlic Granules

2 tablespoons Nutmeg

10 tablespoons Salt

4 teaspoons Curing Salt

4 cups Nonfat Dry Milk

2 cups Water

Directions

(1) Grind meat through a ³/₈ inch grinding plate.

(2) Measure and combine dry ingredients.

(3) Combine meat mixture and dry ingredients in a large container, mixing well. Next, add water, again mixing and kneading thoroughly.

(4) Re-grind mixture through a ³/₈ inch grinding plate.

(5) Stuff seasoned mixture into 2x24-inch *fibrous casings, previously soaked for 20 minutes.*

(6) Cook sausage according to instructions on *pages 65-66.* Sausage is fully cooked when internal temperature reaches 150-155 degrees.

Texas-Style Garlic Bologna

(20 pounds)

12 pounds Lean Beef or Venison
8 pounds Pork Butt
4 tablespoons Onion Flakes
8 tablespoons Garlic Granules
6 teaspoons White Pepper
4 teaspoons Mace
4 teaspoons Yellow Mustard Seed—ground
4 tablespoons Paprika
10 tablespoons Salt
4 teaspoons Cardamon Seed—ground
4 teaspoons Curing Salt
4 cups Nonfat Dry Milk
2 cups Water

Directions

(1) Grind meat through a ³/₈ inch grinding plate.
(2) Measure and combine dry ingredients.
(3) Combine meat mixture and dry ingredients in a large container, mixing well. Next, add water, again mixing and kneading thoroughly.
(4) Re-grind mixture through a ³/₈ inch grinding plate.
(5) Stuff seasoned mixture into 2x24-inch *fibrous casings, previously soaked for 20 minutes.*
(6) Cook sausage according to instructions on *pages 65-66.* Sausage is fully cooked when internal temperature reaches 150-155 degrees.

Texas-Style Pepperoni

(20 pounds)

16 pounds Lean Beef or Venison

3 pounds Pork Butt

1 pound Pork Fat

4 teaspoons Curing Salt

10 tablespoons Salt

2 tablespoons Red Chili Peppers—crushed

2 teaspoons Curry Powder

5 tablespoons Cayenne Pepper

8 tablespoons Anise Seed—whole

1 teaspoon Garlic Powder

1 teaspoon Black Pepper—table grind

4 cups Nonfat Dry Milk

1 cup Water

Directions

(1) Grind meat through a ³/₈ inch grinding plate.

(2) Measure and combine dry ingredients.

(3) Combine meat mixture and dry ingredients in a large container, mixing well. Next, add water, again mixing and kneading thoroughly.

(4) Re-grind mixture through a ³/₈ inch grinding plate.

(5) Stuff seasoned mixture into 2x24-inch *fibrous casings, previously soaked for 20 minutes.*

(6) Cook sausage according to instructions on *pages 65-66.* Sausage is fully cooked when internal temperature reaches 150-155 degrees.

Texas-Style Garlic and Onion Roll

(20 pounds)

16 pounds Lean Beef or Venison

4 pounds Pork Butt

4 tablespoons Onion Granules

8 tablespoons Garlic Granules

4 teaspoons Curing Salt

10 tablespoons Salt

2 teaspoons Marjoram

2 cups Onions—chopped

2 teaspoons Ginger

2 teaspoons Mace

4 cups Nonfat Dry Milk

2 cups Water

Directions

(1) Grind meat through a ³/₈ inch grinding plate.

(2) Measure and combine dry ingredients.

(3) Combine meat mixture and dry ingredients in a large container, mixing well. Next, add water, again mixing and kneading thoroughly.

(4) Re-grind mixture through a ³/₈ inch grinding plate.

(5) Stuff seasoned mixture into 2x24-inch *fibrous casings, previously soaked for 20 minutes.*

(6) Cook sausage according to instructions on *pages 65-66.* Sausage is fully cooked when internal temperature reaches 150-155 degrees.

Texas Jalapeño Roll

(20 pounds)

14 pounds Lean Beef or Venison

6 pounds Pork Butt

10 tablespoons Salt

4 teaspoons Curing Salt

4 tablespoons Jalapeño Pepper Flakes

2 tablespoons Red Chili Pepper—crushed

1 cup Fresh Jalapeño—remove seeds and dice

4 tablespoons Paprika

4 teaspoons Allspice

3 teaspoons Garlic Powder

2 cups Nonfat Dry Milk

2 cups Water

Directions

(1) Grind meat through a ³⁄₈ grinding plate.

(2) Measure and combine dry ingredients.

(3) Combine meat mixture and dry ingredients in a large container, mixing well. Next, add water, again mixing and kneading thoroughly.

(4) Re-grind mixture through a ³⁄₈ inch grinding plate.

(5) Stuff seasoned mixture into 2x24-inch *fibrous casings, previously soaked for 20 minutes.*

(6) Cook sausage according to instructions on *pages 65-66.* Sausage is fully cooked when internal temperature reaches 150–155 degrees.

Texas-Style Pepper Roll

(20 pounds)

16 pounds Lean Beef or Venison

4 pounds Pork Butt

4 teaspoons Curing Salt

4 tablespoons Celery Seed—whole

15 tablespoons Coarse Black Pepper

10 tablespoons Salt

8 tablespoons Onion Flakes

5 tablespoons Paprika

2 tablespoons Garlic Granules

$^1/_2$ cup Green Bell Pepper—fresh, diced

4 cups Nonfat Dry Milk

2 cups Water

Directions

(1) Grind meat through a $^3/_8$ inch grinding plate.

(2) Measure and combine dry ingredients.

(3) Combine meat mixture and dry ingredients in a large container, mixing well. Next, add water, again mixing and kneading thoroughly.

(4) Re-grind mixture through a $^3/_8$ inch grinding plate.

(5) Stuff seasoned mixture into 2x24-inch *fibrous casings, previously soaked for 20 minutes.*

(6) Cook sausage according to instructions on *pages 65-66.* Sausage is fully cooked when internal temperature reaches 150-155 degrees.

Texas-Style Honey and Brown Sugar Roll

(20 pounds)

16 pounds Lean Beef or Venison
4 pounds Pork Butt
3/4 cup Honey
1/4 cup Brown Sugar
4 teaspoons Curing Salt
10 tablespoons Salt
2 tablespoons Celery Seed—ground
2 tablespoons Coriander—ground
2 tablespoons White Pepper
2 tablespoons Coarse Black Pepper
2 cups Nonfat Dry Milk
2 cups Water

Directions

(1) Grind meat through a 3/8 inch grinding plate.
(2) Measure and combine dry ingredients.
(3) Combine meat mixture and dry ingredients in a large container, mixing well. Next, add water, again mixing and kneading thoroughly.
(4) Re-grind mixture through a 3/8 grinding plate.
(5) Stuff seasoned mixture into 2x24-inch *fibrous casings, previously soaked for 20 minutes.*
(6) Cook sausage according to instructions on *pages 65-66.* Sausage is fully cooked when internal temperature reaches 150-155 degrees.

Italian-Style Salami

(20 pounds)

16 pounds Lean Beef or Venison

4 pounds Pork Butt

10 tablespoons Salt

4 teaspoons Curing Salt

$^1/_2$ cup Dried Bell Pepper Flakes

2 tablespoons Red Chili Pepper—crushed

2 tablespoons Cardamon Seed—ground

8 tablespoons Fennel Seed—whole

4 tablespoons Whole Peppercorn

1 teaspoon Garlic Powder

2 cups Nonfat Dry Milk

2 cups Water

Directions

(1) Grind meat through a $^3/_8$ inch ginding plate.

(2) Measure and combine dry ingredients.

(3) Combine meat mixture and dry ingedients in a large container, mixing well. Next, add water, again mixing and kneading thoroughly.

(4) Re-grind mixture through a $^3/_8$ inch grinding plate.

(5) Stuff seasoned mixture into 2x24-inch *fibrous casings, previously soaked for 20 minutes.*

(6) Cook sausage according to instructions on *pages 65-66.* Sausage is fully cooked when internal temperature reaches 150-155 degrees.

Texas-Style Wieners

(10 pounds)

5 pounds Lean Beef or Venison
5 pounds Pork Butt
2 teaspoons Curing Salt
5 tablespoons Salt
1 tablespoon Mustard Seed—ground
1 tablespoon Ginger
2 tablespoons White Pepper
3 tablespoons Garlic Granules
2 tablespoons Mace
1 tablespoon Coriander
2 cups Nonfat Dry Milk
1 cup Water

For a smaller batch, reduce the recipe by half.
Sheep casings are best suited for wieners.

Directions

(1) Grind meat through a ³/₈ inch grinding plate.

(2) Measure and combine dry ingredients.

(3) Combine meat mixture and dry ingredients in a large container, mixing well. Next, add water, again mixing and kneading thoroughly.

(4) Re-grind meat mixture through a ¹/₈ inch grinding plate.

(5) Stuff meat mixture into sheep casings. Twist and tie-off into 6-inch links.

(6) Precook wieners according to *pages 65-66*.

(7) Fry, boil, grill or broil, as you would any wiener.

Texas-Style "Copycat Slim Jims"

(5 pounds)

4 pounds Lean Beef or Venison
1 pound Pork Butt
2½ tablespoons Salt
1 teaspoon Curing Salt
1½ teaspoons White Pepper
1½ teaspoons Nutmeg
1½ teaspoons Celery Powder
1½ teaspoons Curry Powder
2 teaspoons Black Pepper—table grind
2 teaspoons Garlic Powder
1 tablespoon Liquid Smoke
½ cup Nonfat Dry Milk
½ cup Water

Sheep casings are better suited for these smaller links.

Directions

(1) Grind meat and pork through a ⅜ inch grinding plate.

(2) Combine meat mixture with dry ingredients and mix well. Next, add water and Liquid Smoke, mixing thoroughly.

(3) Re-grind mixture through a ⅛ inch grinding plate.

(4) Stuff seasoned mixture into sheep casings. Twist and tie-off into 12-inch links.

(5) Cook "Copycat Slim Jims" according to the instructions on *pages 65-66*. Meat is completely cooked when the internal temperature reaches 150-155 degrees.

(6) Do not shower in cold bath after removing from the oven. When they have shriveled and are cool to the touch, they are ready to eat.

Texas-Style Pepperoni "Copycat Slim Jims"

(5 pounds)

4 pounds Lean Beef or Venison
1 pound Pork Butt
1 teaspoon Curing Salt
2$\frac{1}{2}$ tablespoons Salt
2 teaspoons Black Pepper—table grind
2 teaspoons Garlic Powder
1 tablespoon Liquid Smoke
2 tablespoons Cayenne Pepper
1 tablespoon Anise Seed—whole
$\frac{1}{2}$ teaspoon Allspice
$\frac{1}{2}$ cup Nonfat Dry Milk
$\frac{1}{2}$ cup Water

Sheep casings are better suited for these smaller links.

Directions

(1) Grind meat and pork through a $\frac{3}{8}$ inch grinding plate.

(2) Combine meat mixture with dry ingredients and mix well. Next, add water and Liquid Smoke and mix thoroughly.

(3) Re-grind mixture through $\frac{1}{8}$ inch grinding plate.

(4) Stuff seasoned mixture into sheep casings. Twist and tie-off into 12-inch links.

(5) Cook "Copycat Slim Jims" according to the instructions on *pages 65-66*. Meat is completely cooked when the internal temperature reaches 150-155 degrees.

(6) Do not shower in cold water after removing from oven. When they have shriveled and are cool to the touch, they are ready to eat.

Texas-Style Jalapeño "Copycat Slim Jim"

(5 pounds)

4 pounds Lean Beef or Venison

1 pound Pork Butt

2$\frac{1}{2}$ tablespoons Salt

1 teaspoon Curing Salt

1 tablespoon Paprika

1 teaspoon Allspice

1 teaspoon Garlic Granules

2 tablespoons Jalapeño Powder

3 tablespoons Fresh Jalapeño—remove seeds and dice

2 teaspoons Black Pepper—table grind

1 teaspoon Liquid Smoke

$\frac{1}{2}$ cup Nonfat Dry Milk

$\frac{1}{2}$ cup Water

Sheep casings are better suited for these smaller links.

Directions

(1) Grind meat and pork through a $\frac{3}{8}$ inch grinding plate.

(2) Combine meat mixture with dry ingredients and mix well. Next, add water and Liquid Smoke and mix thoroughly.

(3) Re-grind mixture through a $\frac{1}{8}$ inch grinding plate.

(4) Stuff seasoned mixture into sheep casings. Twist and tie-off into 12-inch links.

(5) Cook "Copycat Slim Jims" according to the instructions on *pages 65-66*. Meat is completely cooked when the internal temperature reaches 150-155 degrees.

(6) Do not shower in cold water after removing from oven. When they have shriveled and are cool to the touch, they are ready to eat.

CHAPTER 4
General Recipes

Friends and relatives will be humbly amazed with your true cooking skills when served any of the following delicious recipes of hors d'oeuvres or complete meals using your own homemade meats.

Sausage and Cabbage Soup

(Serves 4)

Sauté:

1 large Onion—sliced
1$\frac{1}{2}$ tablespoons Butter
1 small head of Cabbage (about $\frac{3}{4}$ lb.)—grated or sliced

Bring to boil 4 cups beef stock and add sautéed cabbage and onion. To this, add the following ingredients:

1 teaspoon Pepper
1 pound German-Style Link Sausage—
    sliced into 1-1$\frac{1}{2}$ inch slices
1 teaspoon Paprika

Simmer for 20 minutes. Serve with double-crust French bread.

German Sausage and "Karloffelklosse" (Potato Dumplings)

(Serves 4)

Bring to boil 1 cup water in skillet. Place 1 link sausage in water and simmer until cooked thoroughly. Remove from heat and set aside.

Dumplings:

Boil 6 medium peeled potatoes. Let cool and mash. Add:

2 Eggs

1 1/2 teaspoons Salt

1/2 cup Flour

Beat batter until smooth. Roll into balls about 1 1/2 inches in diameter. Drop balls into gently boiling salt water and cook about 10 minutes. Drain well. When ready to serve, melt 1/2 cup butter and pour over dumplings or make a brown gravy and pour over dumplings. Place dumplings on a plate with a portion of cooked sausage.

Ginger Smoky Links and Pfannkuchen (German Pancakes)

(Serves 4)

Place 12 Ginger Smoky Links onto a cookie sheet and brown in a preheated oven at 350 degrees for 5 minutes. Combine and stir until smooth:

3 beaten Eggs
2 tablespoons Corn Starch
$\frac{1}{3}$ cup Warm Water
$\frac{1}{4}$ cup Warm Milk
$\frac{3}{4}$ teaspoon Salt
1 tablespoon Sugar
1 grated rind from a small Lemon

Beat 4–5 egg whites until very stiff. Fold into the above mixture.

In a preheated, heavy 10-inch skillet, melt 2 tablespoons butter. Pour pancake mixture into the skillet and cook over medium heat for 5 minutes or until batter is set, then place into a preheated oven of 400 degrees until pancakes are well puffed. Sprinkle with powdered sugar and serve with smoky links.

Sausage-Stuffed Green Bell Peppers

(Serves 4)

Preheat oven to 350 degrees. Cut tops off of 4 bell peppers and remove seeds. Melt in a saucepan 2 tablespoons of butter, then add sausage and onion, sautéing until *brown*.

$^1/_2$ pound Farmer's Pan Sausage
·3 tablespoons Minced Onion

Add:
1 cup Hot Boiled Rice
2 beaten Eggs
$^1/_4$ teaspoon Paprika
$^1/_4$ teaspoon Worcestershire Sauce
$^1/_2$ teaspoon Salt

Fill bell peppers with mixture and bake in 350-degree preheated oven for about 10-15 minutes.

Sausage-Stuffed Baked Potatoes

(Serves 6)

Cut 6 baked potatoes in half lengthwise and scoop out pulp. Place pulp in a large bowl and add:

½ pound Cooked Sausage—casing removed
3 tablespoons Butter
3 tablespoons Hot Cream
1 teaspoon Salt
2 tablespoons Onion—grated and sautéed
1 tablespoon Horseradish

Beat ingredients until smooth. Whip 2 egg whites until stiff and fold them into potato mixture. Fill potato shell with mixture and top with your favorite grated cheese. Broil under low heat until brown. Serve while hot.

Italian Sausage Marinara Sauce

(Serves 4)

Sauté lightly:
2 tablespoons Olive Oil
1 clove Garlic—minced
1 pound Old-Fashioned Italian Sausage—casing removed

Add slowly:
2 $\frac{1}{2}$ cups Canned Tomatoes—diced

Stir in:
6 Anchovies—finely chopped, and the oil from the anchovies
$\frac{1}{2}$ teaspoon Oregano
1 tablespoon Parsley—chopped

Bring to boil, then reduce heat and simmer for 15-20 minutes, stirring occasionally. Pour over pasta and top with grated Parmesan or Romano cheese.

Baked Gefullter Krautkopf (Stuffed Cabbage)

(Serves 4)

Dip cabbage head into boiling water to soften and loosen the leaves, 3-4 at a time, removing them as you go. Continue dipping and removing leaves until you have the desired amount for your meal.

Soak in water for 2 minutes: 3 one-inch-thick slices of bread. Press out water and combine bread with:

1 pound Kielbasa Sausage—casing removed
1 Egg—beaten
$\frac{1}{2}$ cup Onions—chopped
$\frac{1}{4}$ cup Parsley—chopped
1 teaspoon grated rind of Lemon

Place a portion of the mixture onto a flat cabbage leaf and roll into a log. Secure with a toothpick at each end. Once all of the cabbage leaves are filled and secured, place the rolls snugly in a single layer, into a casserole dish until the dish is filled. Remove the toothpicks and pour 2 cups of boiled cabbage sauce over the rolls. Bake for 35-40 minutes in a 300-degree oven. Serve while hot.

Sausage Kebabs

(Serves 6)

6 wooden or metal Skewers
12 Cherry Tomatoes
12 Pearl Onions
18 Red New Potatoes
2 Bell Peppers
12 Mushroom Caps
1 Link Sausage (any type)—sliced into 1¼-inch pieces

Alternate and place on each skewer:
2 Cherry Tomatoes
2 Pearl Onions
3 Red New Potatoes
3 Bell Pepper slices
2 Mushroom Caps
5 pieces of Link Sausage

Place filled kebab skewers in a shallow container and marinate for 1 hour with the following ingredients:

¼ cup Worcestershire Sauce
¼ cup Teriyaki Sauce
1 tablespoon Garlic

Place on a barbecue grill over simmering coals until brown (about 15-20 minutes), turning occasionally.

Liver Sausage Paté

(Serves 8)

1 pound German Liverwurst Sausage
1 medium Onion—finely chopped
2 Garlic Cloves—minced
1 teaspoon Coarse Black Pepper
2 tablespoons Parsley Flakes
3 tablespoons Brandy or Port Wine
$\frac{1}{8}$ cup Flour
1 Egg

Combine all ingredients and mix well. Sprinkle with crumbled bacon and serve on $\frac{1}{4}$-inch slices of French bread that has been toasted on both sides.

Sausage-Stuffed Jalapeño

(Makes 24)

$^1/_2$ pound Sage Breakfast Sausage
2 cups Bisquick
1 package Shake-N-Bake (pork)
6 Jalapeño Peppers (large)
12 Cheddar Cheese Wedges ($^1/_4$ inch each)
$^1/_4$ cup Water

Combine breakfast sausage and Bisquick together and knead until well mixed. Add water and continue kneading. Roll out dough mixture into individual 4-inch patties at $^1/_8$ inch thick. Slice jalapeño peppers lengthwise and remove seeds. Place a cheese wedge into each pepper half and roll in individual dough patties, pressing ends closed. Roll stuffed dough in Shake-N-Bake, coating well.

Place onto cookie sheet and bake at 350 degrees for 20 minutes.

Chorizo and Egg

(Serves 3)

2 6-inch Chorizo Links
3 tablespoons Diced Onions
2 tablespoons Vegetable Oil
4 Whole Eggs
$\frac{1}{8}$ cup Milk
6 Flour Tortillas

In an iron skillet, combine oil, chorizo, and onions and slow-fry until fully cooked. In a bowl, add milk and eggs, beating well. Pour egg mixture into the precooked chorizo and stir until eggs are scrambled and fully cooked.

Heat tortillas until warm and place several spoonfuls of chorizo and egg onto tortilla, adding your favorite salsa. Fold filled tortillas; serve with re-fried beans and Spanish rice. Eat and enjoy!

Boudin Sausage and Dirty Rice

(Serves 4)

4 6-inch links Boudin
$^3/_4$ cup Chopped Onion
$1^1/_2$ pounds Ground Hamburger Meat
1 tablespoon Olive Oil
$^1/_2$ teaspoon Garlic Powder
1 teaspoon Salt
$^1/_4$ teaspoon Oregano
$^1/_4$ teaspoon Thyme
$^1/_8$ teaspoon Pepper
1 8-ounce can Cream of Mushroom Soup
1 8-ounce can Chicken with Rice Soup
$1^1/_2$ cups Cooked Rice
2 Bay Leaves

Slow simmer Boudin Sausage in 1 inch of water for 5 minutes and set aside. Brown meat and onion in olive oil and add garlic powder, oregano, thyme, salt, pepper, and bay leaves. Simmer for 2–3 minutes. Add both mushroom and chicken soups. Stir well and add rice. Reduce heat and simmer for 5 minutes until rice fluffs. Circle Boudin Sausage on a platter with Dirty Rice mixture in the center.

Cajun Creole Sausage with Red Beans and Rice

(Serves 4)

1¹/₂ pounds Cajun Creole Sausage
1 cup Water

Simmer sausage for 20 minutes in an iron skillet containing 1 inch of water. Turn occasionally until browned on both sides and set aside.

5 cups Red Beans—precooked
5 cups Rice—precooked
3 cups Bean Juice
1 small Garlic Clove—minced
1 tablespoon Salt
I teaspoon Cayenne Pepper
I teaspoon Paprika
1 Bay Leaf
¹/₂ cup Green Bell Pepper—diced
5 tablespoons Olive Oil
1 small Onion—diced

In a large skillet, on low heat, pour in olive oil, garlic, salt, diced bell pepper and onion, sautéing until tender.

Add bean juice, beans, and rice and simmer for 5 minutes. Add cayenne pepper, paprika and bay leaf, continuing to simmer for 5 more minutes.

Remove from heat and serve on a plate with Creole Sausage.

Sausage and Peppers

(Serves 4)

4 medium Red Bell Peppers
4 teaspoons Olive Oil
1 1/2 pounds Polish, German or Kielbasa Sausage
2 cups Onion—sliced
4 Garlic Cloves—minced
1/2 cup White Wine
1/2 teaspoon Rosemary—crushed
1/4 teaspoon Pepper
1/4 teaspoon Salt

Place bell peppers on a cookie sheet and broil until charred on all sides. Let cool. Remove stems and seeds and cut into thin strips. Set aside.

Heat olive oil in a 10-inch iron skillet and add sausage links. Cook over medium heat, turning occasionally until browned on all sides (about 5-6 minutes). Add onions and garlic, sautéing until tender (2-3 minutes). Stir in roasted bell peppers, wine, rosemary, salt and pepper and reduce heat to low, allowing the ingredients to simmer for 5-6 minutes.

Poor Texan's Goulash

(Serves 4)

1 large Onion
1 tablespoon Butter
1 teaspoon Paprika
5 Potatoes—peeled and diced
4 ounces Tomato Paste
$\frac{1}{2}$ small Bell Pepper
$\frac{1}{2}$ teaspoon Salt
1 cup Water
1$\frac{1}{2}$ pounds Sausage—German, Polish or Kielbasa

Sauté onions and butter in a large pot. Add paprika, potatoes, tomato paste, water, salt and pepper. Simmer (partially covered) over low heat for about 30 minutes, occasionally stirring. Add sausage and cook over medium heat for 10 minutes.

Polish Reuben Casserole

(Serves 6)

2 10-ounce cans Cream of Mushroom Soup
1⅓ cups Milk
½ cup Onions—chopped
1 tablespoon Mustard
2 16-ounce cans Sauerkraut—drained
8 ounces Noodles—medium-size, uncooked
1½ pounds Polish Sausage
2 cups Swiss Cheese—shredded
¾ cup Bread Crumbs
2 tablespoons Butter—melted

Preheat oven to 350 degrees. Combine soup, milk, onion, and mustard in a large bowl, mixing well. Spread sauerkraut onto the bottom of a greased 13x9-inch glass baking dish. Cover with uncooked noodles. Spoon soup mixture evenly across the top and add sausage and cheese across the top of this. Combine breadcrumbs and melted butter in a small bowl, mixing well. Sprinkle over sausage and cheese. Cover with foil and bake for 1 hour at 350 degrees.

Salami Pie

(Serves 4)

1 pound Fresh Salami—thinly sliced
1 pound Monterey Jack Cheese—diced into cubes
2 packages Crescent Dough
3 Eggs—beaten
¼ cup Parmesan Cheese—grated

Spread 1 package of the crescent dough along the bottom of a 13x9x2-inch pan. Place salami slices on the dough and sprinkle with Monterey Jack cheese cubes. Combine beaten eggs and Parmesan cheese, mixing well. Spread egg mixture over the Monterey Jack cheese and place remaining package of crescent roll dough over the top. Bake at 325-350 degrees for 30 minutes.

Potato Salad and Bockwurst

(Serves 6)

3 pounds medium Red Potatoes
½ pound Fresh Bockwurst—cooked and
   cut into ⅛ inch-thick slices
½ cup Celery—diced
½ cup Green Onions—sliced
8 leaves Romaine Lettuce
2 tablespoons Parsley Flakes

DRESSING:
6 tablespoons White Wine
2 tablespoons Tarragon Vinegar
½ teaspoon Dijon Mustard
½ teaspoon Salt
½ teaspoon Coarse Ground Black Pepper
¾ cup Olive Oil
Mix dressing ingredients well and set aside.

Cook potatoes in boiling water until tender, about 15-20 minutes. Drain off water and let cool. Cut potatoes into ¼-inch-thick slices and place in a large bowl. Add cooked Bockwurst, celery, green onions, and parsley, tossing gently. Pour dressing over potato mixture, again tossing gently. Serve while warm on top of a bed of lettuce leaves.

Sauerkraut and Bratwurst

(Serves 4)

1 medium Onion—diced
1 quart Sauerkraut
1 Bay Leaf
1½ pounds Bratwurst—cut into ½-inch slices
1 teaspoon Caraway Seeds
1 teaspoon Butter

Melt butter in a large skillet, adding onion, bay leaf, and caraway seeds. Sauté for 2 minutes. Add Bratwurst and continue to sauté for 3 minutes or until Bratwurst is browned. Add sauerkraut with juice and cook on low heat for 20 minutes.

Swedish Meatballs

(Serves 4)

$^1\!/_2$ cup Barbecue sauce
$^1\!/_2$ cup Apricot Preserves
1 pound Swedish Sausage—casing removed
1 pound Hamburger
2 tablespoons Green Onions—diced
2 tablespoons Fresh Parsley—diced
2 cups Bread Crumbs
2 Whole Eggs
3 tablespoons Olive Oil

Combine in a large bowl the Swedish Sausage, hamburger meat, green onions, parsley, bread crumbs, and eggs. Mix thoroughly and roll into 1-inch balls.

Heat olive oil in an iron skillet and cook meatballs until browned (about 6-10 minutes). Place meatballs in a casserole dish and set aside.

Sauce: Mix the barbecue sauce and apricot preserves in a bowl and pour over meatballs. Bake at 350 degrees for 45 minutes.

Zucchini Stuffed with Sausage

(Serves 4)

3 medium Zucchini Squash
1 pound Fresh Farmer's Pan Sausage
4 ounces Tomato Paste
1 teaspoon Salt
1 teaspoon Lemon Juice
1 teaspoon Garlic Powder
1 teaspoon Pepper

Combine in a large bowl: Farmer's Pan Sausage, tomato paste, salt and pepper. Mix thoroughly and set aside. Slice zucchini in half, lengthwise. Using a tablespoon, scoop out the zucchini meat, leaving the skin and shell about $1/4$ inch thick. Combine zucchini meat with sausage mixture and mix thoroughly. Stuff zucchini shells with mixture and sprinkle with garlic powder, pouring a small amount of lemon juice across each. Place in a casserole dish and bake at 350 degrees for about 15 minutes. Remove from oven and garnish with your favorite Marinara Sauce.

Sausage Meat-Loaf

(Serves 4)

1$\frac{1}{2}$ pounds Old-Fashioned Sage Sausage
$\frac{3}{4}$ cup Oats
2 Eggs—beaten
$\frac{1}{4}$ cup Onions—diced
$\frac{1}{4}$ teaspoon Pepper
1 cup Tomato Sauce
1 teaspoon Salt

Combine in a large bowl: Sausage, oats, eggs, onions, salt and pepper. Mix thoroughly. Pack mixture into a loaf pan and pour tomato sauce over the mixture. Bake in oven at 350 degrees for about 45 minutes.

Cheese-Rice and Sausage

(Serves 4)

1½ pounds Texas-Style Venison and Bacon Sausage
3 cups Water
1 tablespoon Butter
1 tablespoon Salt
1½ cups Uncooked Rice
2 cups American Cheese—shredded
2 tablespoons Onions—chopped
1 teaspoon Mustard

In an iron skillet of boiling water, sauté the whole link of sausage for about 25-30 minutes and set aside. Bring 3 cups of water to boil in a pot and add butter, salt, and rice. Reduce heat to medium-low and simmer for 20-25 minutes or until rice is tender. Stir cheese, onions, and mustard into hot rice and spread mixture evenly on large serving platter, placing the sausage link on top. Serve while hot.

Chicken and Sausage Jambalaya

(Serves 4)

1 pound Sausage—Polish, German or Kielbasa,
    cut into 1-inch slices
1 pound Chicken Breast—boneless and diced
2 medium White Onions—diced
1 large Green Bell Pepper
10 Green Onions—diced
1 16-ounce can Tomato Sauce
3 large Tomatoes—diced
2 cups Rice—uncooked
3 cloves Garlic—minced
2 teaspoons Cayenne Pepper
2 teaspoons Salt
2 teaspoons Pepper
2 tablespoons Olive Oil
Water

Heat olive oil in a large skillet and add chicken and
salt and pepper, sautéing until cooked. In a large
boiling pot, add chicken, sausage, onions, bell pepper, green onions, tomatoes, garlic, cayenne pepper,
salt and pepper. Add enough water to cover ingredients and cook over low heat for about 10 minutes.
Add rice and tomato sauce to the boiling pot and
cook over medium heat until the rice is tender.

Sausage Queso Dip

2 pounds Velveeta Cheese
1 pound Breakfast Sausage
6 Green Onions—diced
1 6-ounce can Rotel Spicy Tomatoes with Peppers
2 tablespoons Cilantro
½ cup Milk

Sauté breakfast sausage in a skillet until fully cooked. Combine the following ingredients in a large (microwaveable) bowl: sausage, cheese, green onion, Rotel, cilantro, and milk. Place in a microwave for about 3 minutes; remove and stir well and place back in the microwave until completely melted. Remove and stir. Serve with tortilla chips.

Greek Meatballs with Yogurt and Feta Sauce

(Makes 20 meatballs)

1 pound Greek–Style Sausage—casing removed
$^1/_2$ cup Fresh Parsley—chopped
1 Whole Egg
$^1/_4$ cup Bread Crumbs
2 Garlic Cloves—minced
$^1/_2$ teaspoon Salt
$^1/_4$ teaspoon Ground Black Pepper
1 tablespoon Olive Oil

In a large bowl, mix together meat, parsley, egg, bread crumbs, garlic, salt and pepper. Shape into 1-inch balls and set aside. Heat olive oil in a large skillet, adding meatballs and cooking over medium-low heat (stirring occasionally) for about 12 -15 minutes or until thoroughly cooked.

Yogurt/Feta Sauce:
1 4-ounce package Feta Cheese—crumbled
$^3/_4$ cup Plain Yogurt
2 tablespoons Milk
1 Garlic Clove—minced
$^1/_3$ cup Tomato—chopped and seeded
$^1/_3$ cup Cucumber—peeled
1 teaspoon Fresh Dill—finely chopped

Place in a blender: Feta cheese, yogurt, milk and garlic, blending until smooth. Stir in tomato, cucumber, and dill. Pour over sausage balls and serve.

Glossary

Casing Storage: To prolong the shelf life, any remaining pork or sheep casings should be packed in a salt-water solution and stored in a freezer bag with a locking zipper. Keep frozen until needed. When ready to use, thaw, rinse, and soak in cold water in refrigerator overnight.

Cheese (in sausage making): Mild Cheddar or aged Colby should be used for best results. Dice and freeze twenty-four hours before mixing with seasoned meat and stuffing.

Cold Water Shower/Bath: Once meat is fully cooked and the internal temperature reaches 150-155 degrees, a cold water shower or bath allows the fat to coagulate and prevents meats from shriveling.

Game Tallow: White, fatty-like substance between the flesh and skin, found mostly on the lower back and inside the carcass. Becomes rancid very quickly. *Do not use in sausage.*

Lean Meat: Meat that is 99 percent fat-free.

Meat Thermometer: Special thermometer which, when placed inside cooking meat, will read the internal temperature.

Nonfat Dry Milk: This powdered milk is used in sausage making to help bind the meat together, helping to avoid crumbling. It also allows the meat to retain natural juices during cooking.

Pork Butt: Pork meat that is 80 percent meat and 20 percent fat.

Twisting and Tie-offs: For link sausages, smoky links, and Slim Jims. Twist the casing at designated lengths to separate links. Twist 4-5 turns in one direction and twist 4-5 turns in the opposite direction for the next link. This prevents the casing from unraveling. Tie-off with cotton twine.

Venison: Deer meat. More lean in comparison to beef or pork. Deer meat must be cleaned and cooled as quickly as possible after harvesting.

Water-soaked Wood Chips: This process produces a pungent smoke, allowing a rich, smoke flavor to meats. The dampened wood chips will smoke longer and are less likely to flame and cause meats to burn.